REBORN WITH CREDIT

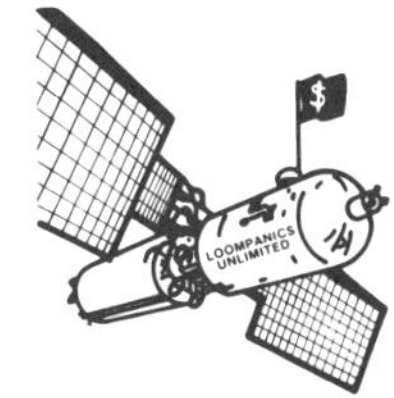

Trent Sands

Loompanics Unlimited
Port Townsend, Washington

These other fine books by Trent Sands are available from Loompanics Unlimited:

- Reborn in the U.S.A. (Expanded Second Edition)
- Reborn in Canada (Expanded Second Edition)
- Reborn Overseas

This book is sold for information purposes only. Neither the author nor the publisher will be held accountable for the use or misuse of the information contained in this book.

Reborn With Credit

Published by:

Loompanics Unlimited
P.O. Box 1197
Port Townsend, WA 98368

Loompanics Unlimited is a division of Loompanics Enterprises, Inc.

ISBN 1-55950-090-5
Library of Congress Catalog Card Number 91-Pending

Contents

Introduction

Each year, thousands of people find themselves unable to obtain credit because in the past they have had credit problems, or because they have never established credit. Most of the time these rejected people have no idea of what, if anything, they can do to either establish good credit or to remove bad credit. The reason for this is the credit system is cloaked in secrecy, and the credit grantors want it to remain that way. Paradoxically, the credit system many times works in a backwards fashion. We have all heard stories about the teenager who was able to order an American Express Card through the mail, or we have friends who have a low income, who have received "pre-approved" offers for credit cards. By the same token, were the reader with a good income to apply for that very same card, a rejection letter would be sent.

This book will lay out step-by-step what anyone must do to obtain the credit they deserve. Your previous credit situation makes no difference. Follow the methods outlined and you will shortly have the credit you need in life.

1

Credit Basics

The credit system involves three principal groups. The first group consists of "creditors": the financial institutions and stores that offer credit products to the public. These products range from department store charge cards to bankcards to home mortgages. The second group is the consumers or, in credit industry terms, the "applicants." Needless to say, this group is the key to the credit industry profits. The third group is the credit bureau network. They earn their money by selling their services to creditors.

The credit bureau acts like a referee in the credit system. Their job is to verify the information that is put onto a credit application. It was not always like this. There was a time when all creditors would contact directly any references listed on an application and confirm the details themselves. The creditor would call the applicant's employer, bank and landlord and ask each of them about their experiences with the applicant. In those days, the role of the credit bureau was much different than it is today.

Credit bureaus started as a way for local merchants to protect themselves from people who would open charge accounts and never pay back the money they owed. In the late 1950s, many local stores offered charge accounts to their regular customers. Generally, the customer would fill out a file card at the store listing his or her full name, birthdate, home address, telephone number and employer along with a local personal reference. This file card would go upstairs to the credit office and the store would call the applicant's employer and bank. Having obtained satisfactory verification, the applicant would then receive charging privileges at the store.

Merchant Protection Associations

Credit bureaus became a part of the picture when local merchants realized that in a given city it was the same small number of people who were not paying their accounts on time. At this time, local credit bureaus were called "Merchant Protection Associations," and the name was accurate. The names of deadbeats were kept on file at the MPA and whenever a person applied for credit, the merchant would make sure that the person was not on file with the MPA. So we can see that at the very beginning credit bureaus were designed to be just a negative database that the majority of people never had any contact with.

It didn't take long for merchants to see the other side to the local protection association. If having the names of bad credit risks enabled a store to increase profits by keeping losses to a minimum, what about doing the very same with good credit risks? By reporting the names of on-time payers to the local credit bureau, preferred customers could be contacted by merchants directly and offered charge accounts. The bureaus were cost effective for merchants because the time consuming business of reference checking could be dispensed with entirely. The very fact that these people were on record at the MPA as good payers was proof enough to open a charge account. So here we have the beginnings of pre-approved credit!

National Credit Bureaus

Merchant protection associations were still local operations, and a consumer who did not have good credit in one town could still get credit in another town. But big changes were underway. Larger credit bureaus started buying up smaller ones, and a massive switchover from paper records to computer records was occurring at the same time. In these early days, most computers were expensive mainframes, and this is the primary reason that the industry developed as it did.

Large mainframe computers could only be afforded by a few companies. An industry grew up that rented computer time to small organizations that could not afford their own computers. One such company that provided computing services to other firms was TRW. This company is now the largest of the four main credit bureaus in the country.

TRW started to buy up many of the smaller credit bureaus and put on its network those that would not allow themselves to be purchased. The end result was one giant credit database. Local bureaus agreed to send copies of their records to TRW's central computer. In return, TRW provided information to the local bureaus on applicants the locals had no files on. For example, if a person moved into an area served by one of these local bureaus from another state, no local credit file would exist on that person. The local, TRW-affiliated credit bureau would then call TRW with the particulars on this individual, and TRW would search its files for information. In a few days, this information would be relayed back to the local credit bureau. This was the beginning of the nationwide credit reporting system we now have.

Another group was also getting into the credit bureau industry: the traditional investigative companies that worked for the insurance industry. These companies specialized in performing what can best be called lifestyle reports on applicants for insurance. Thc largest of these companies is called Equifax, now known by its new name, Credit Bureau Incorporated, or CBI. This company is based in Atlanta and has files on about forty million people.

The other major national credit bureaus are Trans Union Credit and CSC (formerly, ACS). Credit bureaus also have a trade association, known as Associated Credit Bureaus, or ACB. The addresses for the bureaus and ACB are shown below:

TRW Credit Services
505 City Parkway West
Orange, California 92667

CBI/Equifax
P.O. Box 4091
Atlanta, Georgia 30302

Trans Union Credit
444 North Michigan Avenue
Chicago, Illinois 60611

CSC
624 E. North Belt, #400
Houston, Texas 77060

Associated Credit Bureaus
16211 Park Place #10
Houston, Texas 77218

The Rise of the Bankcard

The use and availability of credit cards zoomed in the 1970s. This decade brought with it the general use bankcards such as VISA and Mastercard. Prior to this time a credit card was something most people thought of in connection with a department store or oil company, who used the cards primarily as a way of building customer loyalty. A person who carried one oil company credit card with him could only purchase gas and repairs at that firm's service stations. The same was true for department store shoppers. Often the convenience of credit card shopping would sway a major purchase decision.

About this time some smaller merchants began to band together in a certain city or region and issue a locally-valid charge card that could be used at all of their stores. The card would be issued in conjunction with a local bank that would actually approve the credit applications and do the billings on the accounts. Over time the banks began to realize that there could be enormous profits in an all-purpose credit card that could be used nationwide and have wide acceptability. This is how the modern version of the general purpose bankcard was born. We should look at how a typical bankcard transaction works to explain the system at work.

VISA and Mastercard

The key to bankcard success is widespread acceptability. It does a cardholder little good if he can use his card at only a few places in a given city. This is what the VISA and Mastercard names and symbols are all about. The card is not issued by VISA or Mastercard, but by the bank where the person applied for the card. This bank is a member of either the VISA or Mastercard interbank association. As a member of these associations, the bank is entitled to place these symbols on the credit cards it issues and to have access to the clearing and payment system that the interbank association maintains. The clearing system is what allows one bank to collect payment for the credit card transaction slips that are drawn on other banks.

There was a time when a person could decide that credit was not something they wanted, and live on a cash basis. In today's world, that is almost impossible, and the credit grantors are the reason why. Try to rent a car, reserve a decent hotel room, or travel without a credit card. It is nearly impossible to rent a car without a credit card, and the same is happening with hotels. But it is a double-edged sword. As people must have credit sooner, more of these people will have credit problems later on because they did not appreciate how much debt they had taken on or were careless about making payments. The best way to explain the credit system is to examine it at work on a typical request.

How a Credit Application is Processed

You walk into a restaurant one day and grab a VISA card application from the cashier's counter. While you're waiting for your meal, you fill out the application. The application asks for all sorts of personal information: your name, birth date, Social Security number, last two addresses, bank accounts, work place, etc. After your meal, you mail the application off to the bank which issues this particular VISA card.

The first step in the credit process is what is called "scoring." When your application arrives at the bank, a low-level data processing clerk will enter the information you provided into a computer. The computer has a software program that awards a certain number of "points" for each item on the application. For example, if you own your own home, you will receive more points than someone who rents.

Each financial institution has what is known as its "cut off" point total. If your application scores beneath this number, the bank will waste no more time with your application, and a rejection letter will be sent out to you at once. If your application scores above that number, the bank will order a credit report on you from one or possibly two credit bureaus. The reason the bank does not automatically order credit reports for every applicant is that the bank must pay for each credit report they order. Why waste money buying credit reports on people that don't even meet the bank's minimum lending criteria?

Once the credit report has arrived — often within minutes by on-line computer hook-up — the application and credit report will be sent to a junior "credit analyst" in the credit card department. He or she will examine the credit report to look for any late payments, accounts that had to be written off, or whether the applicant has too much debt. If the credit report largely agrees with what appears on the application, the credit card will be approved. A credit limit will be set, either as a ratio of your gross salary, or as a standard limit set by the bank on all new accounts. A few weeks later, your VISA card arrives through the mail.

Understanding Credit Decisions

To successfully use the credit system, one must understand the credit guarantor's policies and feelings. In the industry, this is called "credit culture." Credit culture answers the question, "What type of people do we want to lend money to?" For example, the credit culture of American Express is certainly different from your local, high interest finance company. American Express wants to lend money only to above average income professional people, who really do not need the money. Your finance company may charge rates like a loan shark, but in a bind, if you are any kind of a decent risk, they will lend you money.

The other part of the system that you must understand is the credit bureau. A bad credit report will destroy any chance to obtain credit; a good credit report will literally have pre-approved applications coming to your doorstep. Until your credit report says on it what you want it to say, you can forget about getting any credit.

2

Credit Bureau Services

Credit Reports

Credit bureau reports contain more personal information on an individual than almost any other database, private or government. Under the "personal information" section, your credit bureau file will contain your name, birth date, Social Security number, last two addresses, and marital status. Under the "employment" section, it will have the name and address of your employer, along with your current salary and length of employment. There is another section on your credit report called "public information." Credit bureaus monitor the local courthouse and the U.S. Bankruptcy Court in your area. They enter into their data files the names of those people who are subject to lawsuits or judgments.

The next part of the credit report contains your actual credit history. Here, there will be a listing of all of your loans and charge accounts, what the current balance is on these accounts, the amount of the minimum payment, your highest balance on the account, and at the side a numerical code that indicates how you pay. This code runs from a zero to a nine. A nine indicates an account was charged off, a one means you pay right on time.

Credit reports differ a little in format from company to company. I suggest you order a copy of your credit report. For about $10 you can get a copy of your report. Look in the Yellow Pages under "Credit Bureaus" or "Credit Reporting Agencies" and send a letter with your name, address, birth date and Social Security number, along with the current fee. In a couple of weeks, you will have a copy of your report. If you have been turned down for credit, the rejection letter you received will tell you where to write for a free copy of your credit report.

Credit Analysis

Credit bureaus have become much more than just idle collectors of information for creditors. They have also become analyzers of financial information. Credit bureaus analyze data using computer software programs. For example, one large credit bureau has a software program that analyzes how quickly a person runs through lines of credit, the person's payment history and income growth, to determine if that person is a likely candidate for bankruptcy. A credit grantor who orders this option on the credit reports they receive will see a notation on the report if the credit bureau software indicates this person is such a candidate.

On the other hand, these same software programs allow many people who should not receive credit cards or lines of credit to get them. A good example is the "pre-approved" credit card offer that comes in the mail. Usually these offers say that because of your financial standing you are being offered an opportunity for a pre-approved credit line, usually between $500 and $1,500, or a pre-approved VISA or Mastercard. All you have to do is sign the request form, and sometimes include your Social Security number or phone number. The offer makes it sound as if you were singled out, but then it turns out that everyone in your neighborhood got the same offer. How does it work?

Banks frequently make use of a credit bureau service called "computer profiling." Let us assume a bank wants to launch a new "Gold" VISA card with a $5,000 credit limit that includes a heavy $65 per year annual fee. The bank can go to the credit bureau and ask for a list of areas of a city where the average annual income is over $45,000, that have a high percentage of homeowners, and whose residents include a lot of professional people. The credit bureau can go through its files using a software program that includes the criteria the bank has asked for. Then, by matching this data up against real estate assessments for the given city, the credit bureau can produce a list of several thousand people in one or two neighborhoods that are very likely to meet these criteria.

Understand that the credit bureau will not actually make sure that all these people have good credit, but the odds are very high that most of them do. To make sure that no one is left out, the credit bureau will use what is known as a telephone criss-cross directory once the geographical boundaries of the target area are identified. A telephone criss-cross directory lists phone numbers by address. The odds are very high that anyone with a listed phone number in the target region will get a pre-approved application. So, a student who happens to rent a basement apartment within this area will very likely receive a gold card application.

3

Fixing Bad Credit

Cleaning up credit reports became big business at the end of the 1980s. In many magazines you will see advertisements that tell you they can clean up your credit, for a fee. The fee starts at several hundred dollars and can go as high as $5,000. You can do the same thing yourself for a few dollars in postage and a little time and effort. An individual can do this because of provisions in the laws that credit bureaus and credit grantors operate under.

The Fair Credit Reporting Act says that if a credit bureau is challenged about an entry on a credit report, they must justify it to the consumer. This justification must come in the form of a confirmation statement from the source of the entry. If the credit bureau cannot furnish the consumer with this confirmation within a reasonable period of time, then the item must be removed from the credit report. Even if the creditor verifies the item at a later date, the credit bureau cannot re-insert it onto the report. Let's look at the various negative items that might be on your credit report, and devise a strategy for removing each one.

Excessive Inquiries

Every time you apply for credit, a notation is made on your credit report that someone inquired about your credit worthiness. People who are denied credit frequently reapply time and time again. Each one of these attempts is shown on the credit report. When the next creditor sees the report, the first question is why should he or she extend credit when no one else will. A lot of inquiries can also trigger the credit bureau's fraud detection programs. There are thousands of people who have destroyed their chances of obtaining credit because they have too many inquiries listed on their report. The good news is, if this is your case, this is the easiest type of credit report problem to repair.

You can proceed according to one of two ways. The first is to dispute the inquiry with the creditor. The second is to dispute the inquiry with the credit bureau. I recommend dealing with the credit bureau. The way you do this is to send a letter to all the major credit bureaus that have the unwanted inquiries on your report. You must send a separate letter to each credit bureau for the inquiries you wish to dispute on their reports. The letter is very simple. The letter should have your name, birthdate, Social Security number and address. On the letter you would say that you have no recollection of that particular inquiry, and would they please investigate it and remove it. Keep a copy of the letter and send it certified mail. A sample letter appears on the next page.

Sample Letter for Disputing Inquiries

Your Name
Your Address
Your City, State, Zip
Soc. Sec. #: XXX-XX-XXXX
Birthdate: XX/XX/XX

Today's Date

Credit Bureau Name
Credit Bureau Address
City, State, Zip

To Whom It May Concern:

I did not authorize the following inquiries on my credit report. Please investigate them and send me a copy of my corrected credit report.

Name of Creditor
Date of Inquiry

Name of Creditor
Date of Inquiry

Name of Creditor
Date of Inquiry

Name of Creditor
Date of Inquiry

Sincerely,
(Signature)
Printed Name

After the letter arrives at the credit bureau a process is put into motion. The credit bureau will pull a copy of your credit report and make sure the inquiry is present. They will then mail a copy of your dispute letter along with a confirmation slip to the creditor in question. The creditor will then check his records to confirm the inquiry. If no confirmation is found, the inquiry must be removed from the credit report. At least this is how it works in theory. The reality is much different.

Confirming an inquiry costs a creditor money. Someone from the credit department must go and search the records for the inquiry. There is nothing to gain for the creditor because, since credit was never granted, no account was opened and no money was lost. A record of the inquiry probably will not exist after 90 days. When no account is established, the creditor generally hangs onto inquiry records for a short time, and then disposes of them. There is a good chance the letter requesting confirmation of the inquiry will simply be ignored.

Five weeks later send the credit bureau a follow up letter like the one shown on the next page. In almost all cases this will be enough to get simple inquiries removed.

Follow-Up Letter for Removing Any Disputed Items or Inquiries

Your Name
Your Address
Your City, State, Zip
Soc. Sec. #: XXX-XX-XXXX
Birthdate: XX/XX/XX

Today's Date

Credit Bureau Name
Credit Bureau Address
City, State, Zip

To Whom It May Concern:

On (date of previous letter) I sent you a letter (copy attached) asking you to investigate and remove the following items from my credit report. You are required by law to remove these items unless you can verify them. Please remove these items and send me a copy of my corrected credit report.

Name of Creditor
Date of Inquiry or Account Number

Name of Creditor
Date of Inquiry or Account Number

Name of Creditor
Date of Inquiry or Account Number

Sincerely,
(Signature)
Printed Name

Charge-Offs

Removing a record of a debt that was written off by the creditor can require more effort. The difference is that in this case the creditor has lost money and has an interest in seeing that your credit is damaged. In short he is angry, and wants to make you suffer in the only way he can. But a persistent campaign will often yield results here. The key aspect of the law to remember is that the first time the creditor fails to confirm a disputed item within a reasonable time period, the credit bureau must remove this item from your report.

There are loopholes in everything. The first loophole is in the records creditors keep. Let's assume that five years ago you had a loan that had to be written off. There is a very good chance that the creditor no longer has the records from this account. Generally, after a three year period, a creditor assumes that an account is totally uncollectible, and it is written off. The account will have been given to a collection agency, and the collection agency may have given up on it.

In this situation there is a very good chance that you will be able to get the disputed account removed. Once again, on such an old account the creditor will not have readily-available records to consult. This will often cause enough delay in the response to allow the item to be removed from the report. You can use the same letter format as shown for disputing inquiries, only you dispute the debt. If you get no response in five weeks, ask for the item to be removed.

Slow-Pays

For accounts that are still open and delinquent, where the creditor does confirm the account, another strategy is available that frequently works. We must first understand the mind of the creditor. To the creditor, you are nothing but a deadbeat that has caused him a loss. If he can reduce that loss by a substantial amount, he will be interested in doing so. This is particularly true of collections departments, whose performance is based on how much they bring in. In these cases the best idea is to write a letter to the creditor, proposing a deal. You will pay off the account, or a sizeable amount, and in return they will agree to remove the negative items from the report.

You would follow the same procedure as before, keeping a copy of all correspondence. Make sure that you get the creditor's firm commitment in writing before you make any payment on the account. The sample letter for doing this is shown on the next page.

Sample Agreement Between You and Creditor

Your Name
Your Address
Your City, State, Zip
Account Number:

Today's Date

Creditor Name
Creditor Address
City, State, Zip

Dear Creditor:

This is in regard to account shown above with an outstanding balance of $. I agree to pay you the sum of $ as payment in full of this obligation, if you agree to remove this item from my credit report and no longer report the delinquency to any credit bureaus.

If you agree to this arrangement, please have a copy of this letter signed by an authorized representative of your company in the space provided below. Return the signed copy of this agreement to me and I will immediately forward payment.

Sincerely,
(Signature)
Printed Name

I agree to the arrangement described above.

____

Name Date

Inserting Explanations

Sometimes there will be an account that you cannot rectify either through an agreement with the creditor or by disputing the item with the credit bureau. If you can remove most of the bad accounts on your credit report, you can generally obtain new credit. For the accounts you can't remove, you are entitled to insert a note of explanation on your credit report that will be seen by all future parties who ask for your report.

Under the Fair Credit Reporting Act, you have the right to include a short statement as to why an item appears on your report. You can use up to 100 words to explain each item on your report. If a person has good credit with the exception of one bad item on the report, and the 100-word explanation is plausible, creditors will assume that the bad item was due to a legitimate dispute. A sample 100-word statement is shown on the next page. You will need to tailor the wording to fit each item on your report.

You should try to think up a good reason for not being able to pay your debts on time. The best reason, as far as creditors are concerned, is an unexpected bill that will not happen again. For example, death in the family requiring a leave from work and an expensive plane trip; an injury that required expensive medical treatment but is not recurring; your car was smashed by an uninsured drunk driver and you had to buy a new one for your work. The key elements to these explanations are that you couldn't have planned for this or done anything to prevent it, and it's not likely to happen again.

Sample Letter to Insert Statement on Report

Your Name
Your Address
Your City, State, Zip
Soc. Sec. #: XXX-XX-XXXX
Birthdate: XX/XX/XX

Today's Date

Credit Bureau Name
Credit Bureau Address
City, State, Zip

To Whom It May Concern:

I would like the following statement of explanation to be inserted on my credit report concerning the item reported by (name of creditor and account number).

In January of 1992 I suffered a severe injury at home. At that time, I was not covered under health insurance. Due to the medical bills, I was unable to pay this creditor in a timely manner. The injury has healed completely and is not a recurring problem. I am now covered by a health insurance policy, so I do not believe this same situation will happen again. I am doing my best to pay all my bills and establish good credit.

Please insert this note of explanation and send me a copy of my revised credit report.

Sincerely,
(Signature)

Printed Name

Bankruptcies, Liens and Other Black Marks

The last type of information that you want to remove is public record information. This type of information includes such things as bankruptcy judgments, wage garnishments and liens placed against you. Serious credit problems like these must be handled a little differently because of the easy availability of confirmation of the particular event. The loophole on these type of judgments is that the confirmation must come from the custodian of the records.

The fact that your name may be listed on the bankruptcy index for a given year at a certain bankruptcy court is not sufficient confirmation. The court clerk must obtain the record of the actual bankruptcy order to confirm the bankruptcy. The following strategy will work when the bankruptcy is a few years old. This works because the actual bankruptcy file will have been sent to a federal archive center. To obtain the record the court clerk will have to order it from the archive.

The first step is to order a copy of your file from the court. The same day that you do this, write to the credit bureau disputing the bankruptcy. The records will be shipped from the archive to the bankruptcy court for your inspection. During this period, the court clerk will not be able to process the credit bureau's request for verification of your bankruptcy.

It will take at least two weeks for your records to be shipped from the archive to the court. Usually, the credit bureau will not have even begun to process your request for confirmation. Do not contact the court to see if your records have arrived; wait for them to contact you before going to copy the documents. While you're stalling, your records will be in a holding area and unavailable for credit bureau confirmation.

While this delay is going on, you send your follow-up letter to the credit bureau requesting deletion of the bankruptcy. Variations of this strategy are very effective in removing all sorts of public record information. Quite often the inertia of the bureaucracy ensures that you can get these items cleared off long before confirmation of the event is received at the credit bureau.

In the next chapter, you will learn how to create a new credit bureau file for yourself that contains no bad information. It does not matter if you have been bankrupt or if you've had repossessions. This method will allow you to obtain a "clean slate." Once this clean slate is obtained at the credit bureau, you can then follow my quick method to get your first loan or credit card.

4
Creating A Blank Slate At The Bureau

The method described in this chapter is useful to the person who wants a clear credit file in their own name or the person who wants to create a new identity from the ground up. This method is known as "File Segregation," "Alternate File Creation," or, as I prefer, "Dummy Credit File" creation. Essentially, creating a dummy credit file allows you to obtain a completely blank file at the credit bureau in your own name. There will be no credit history contained on the new file, but there will not be any negative information either. The next step after this is to start building a favorable credit rating by obtaining new credit, which is explained in the next chapter.

Dummy credit files can be created because of the massive number of files that credit bureaus must maintain. There are thousands of people who have the same first, middle and last names. There are also thousands of people with identical dates of birth. Some people appear to have identical Social Security numbers, caused either by errors made on writing the number down on an application form, or a computer operator entering it incorrectly, or actual duplicate numbers being issued by the Social Security Administration. To reduce the possibility of file mix ups, credit bureaus use one of two ways to create brand new files.

How the Bureaus Make New Files

The first method depends entirely upon the Social Security number. A person of the same name who uses a different social security number will automatically create a new credit file for himself. The second system relies on a code made from parts of the personal identification information. If this code matches an existing credit file, then a new file will not be created. We will examine how the second method works, because if you can generate a new file on this system, the same strategy will work on the other system as well. Once you start a new credit bureau file, it is the one that creditors will judge you by and the one they report your credit history to.

You must create this dummy credit file carefully because the credit bureaus use fraud detection programs to catch this sort of activity. We will talk more about fraud detection software in a later chapter. First, let's look at how the credit bureaus create a new file and what the personal code consists of.

The first part of the code consists of up to the first ten letters of your last name. After the computer brings up these letters of the last name, it will look for an existing match. If it does not find an existing match, a new file will be created. Needless to say, last names are common enough that a match is almost always found. When a match is found at this point, the computer then takes the first three letters of the first name and adds them to the previous last name letters. If no match comes at this point, a new file is created. Most first names are common enough that a match will still be found. At this point the computer adds the middle initial, and tries the same matching technique again. If a match is found it will then check the marital status by adding the spouse's first initial to the string of letters.

This process continues. After the spouse's first initial will come the first five digits of the house number, then the first letters of the street name, then the zip code, and finally the previous address. If everything still matches an existing file, the computer checks the Social Security number. If the Social Security number is different, the credit bureau will open a new credit file, but a fraud warning will appear on it. The bureau assumes that if everything matches an existing file except the Social Security number, someone is trying to pull a fast one.

Many people falsely believe that by just changing the Social Security number and nothing else they can create a new file. That method only works on the first new credit file system mentioned earlier. You can not rely on your credit bureau using the Social Security number system anymore. Even if they use it now, they will probably switch to this more elaborate coding system soon.

Creating a New You

To create a new file in your own name, you will first need to get a new mailing address. You cannot, however, use a mail forwarding service for this purpose. Most of the credit bureau anti-fraud software programs will detect the address of most mail services in a given area. To get your new address, you must use a secretarial service or an office rental service. It will cost a little more than a mail drop, but it avoids problems.

The reason credit bureaus do not flag these secretarial services is that many legitimate companies use them. For example, if a company must keep only three or four people in a region at any time, they will often rent a packaged office or packaged secretarial service. This makes more sense than to spend a lot of money on a full time office. Secretarial service, fax lines and other services are available on an as-needed basis.

The previous address you use should not be one where you really lived. You could safely pull a previous address right off any apartment complex.

You don't need to make up a new last name unless it is a very rare, one-in-a-thousand name. You will, however, transpose your first name with your middle name. Your middle name now becomes your first name. Next, you will make up a new Social Security number. A list of representative number series is given in Appendix 6. And finally you will get a new telephone number in the name where your middle name is now your first. You will now be able to create your new credit file.

Opening a New Credit Bureau File

Go to a credit bureau in your area and ask to see your credit report. They will not have an existing file because of your new name and address information. You will then receive a credit report that is blank except for the basic personal information that you provided to get the report. With this simple request, the credit bureau has now opened a brand-new, blank credit file on you. You have created a clean slate!

From now on, when you apply for credit anywhere, you must give the same personal information you gave the credit bureau: your new name, address, previous address, Social Security number, etc. Then it will be this new, blank file that the creditors will see on your credit report. It should be easy to see that if you are creating a new identity from the ground up, you will also create a new credit file using this method as well.

Establishing a New Credit History

Once your new file is in place you are now ready to get credit. If you are working at a job that creditors consider credit worthy, the procedure is very easy. First, open up a checking account and savings account at a bank. Be sure to give the same mailing address you gave the credit bureau. The next step is to open a savings account at a local credit union. Once this has been done you will want to write away to banks that offer a secured credit card program. A list of several of these banks appears in Appendix 2. You can find others through advertisements in tabloids or magazines.

These banks agree to give you a Mastercard or VISA card in exchange for you making a deposit of at least $500 in an interest-bearing savings account. Your account is frozen, so you can't touch it as long as you have the credit card. Your credit limit is at least 40% of the deposit amount. Many of these banks don't do a credit check, and others only require that there are no bankruptcies on your credit file. They also issue cards to people who have no credit history. The VISA or Mastercard account will appear on your credit file like any credit card account. The only one who will know it is a collateralized card is the bank that issues the card.

The next step in your credit repair course is to accumulate about $750 in your credit union savings account. After you have done this, ask to take out a $500 loan against the account. Five hundred dollars of your savings will be frozen until the loan is paid off. The credit union will be happy to make the loan because it is secured. The most they will do is check to see that you are still employed. Pay off the loan in two installments. You will then have a second credit reference on your new credit file, in addition to your secured credit card.

If you are working in a job that credit grantors don't like, such as a waiter or musician, or if you are creating a new identity, you will need to backstop your new credit report once further with a desirable employment reference. This is easily done by contracting with another office rental or secretarial service. They will answer the telephone in your "company" name and verify your employment as you have instructed them. Following this program, within three months you will be able to obtain credit for almost any purpose.

5

Anti-Fraud Programs

Both creditors and credit bureaus have various means of detecting fraudulent credit applications. In fact, the science of detecting fraud is so advanced that there are several computer programs that banks, credit bureaus and other interested parties can buy that help them detect fraud. These programs are based on an analysis of accounts that have gone bad, focusing on common characteristics on the original application forms that point to problems. In this way, these programs don't only look for fraud, but also for bad credit risks.

Creditor Anti-Fraud Programs

Anyone who accepts credit applications probably has some system for verifying the information they contain. Banks and large retailers have found that the cheapest way to verify the information is to run it through a fraud-detecting computer program. These programs are designed to enable merchants to catch people trying to obtain credit cards fraudulently through false information on the credit application. Using the software is cheaper than personally verifying all the information on the credit application. It is also cheaper than buying a credit report from a credit bureau, which is never done until after the internal fraud detection system is used.

Here are some of the things this software looks for. All bank credit cards listed on the application should start with a four digit number assigned exclusively to the issuing bank. This number is called the bank identification number. All Mastercards start with the digit "5" and all VISA cards start with the digit "4." Oil company credit cards have a common numbering system as do travel and entertainment cards, such as Diners Club and American Express.

There are many other items on the credit application that these fraud detection programs look for. We will cover them in detail in the next chapter, where we will go through a credit application entry-by-entry. For now, let's look at what the credit bureau can use to detect fraudulent applications.

Credit Bureau Anti-Fraud Software

Credit bureaus have come up with a number of detection programs to trip up people who are trying to leave a poor credit history behind. The credit bureaus have introduced computer software programs into their databases in an attempt to detect fraudulent credit applications. When the software discovers a potential fraud, the credit report is tagged with a notation that something is amiss, alerting the creditor to possible fraud.

One of these software programs is called "HAWK." Another is called "CHECKPOINT." The way these programs work is by looking at certain common characteristics of fraudulent accounts. For example, the HAWK program will check an applicant's address against a list of mail forwarding services. If there is a match, the credit report will include a warning of possible fraud. The HAWK program will also check to see if the employer telephone given is legitimate, or if it is the number to a pay phone. It will also check to see if the employer address is a mail receiving address. If these items are not legitimate, then the warning will be placed on the credit report.

Another credit bureau has a program called "SHERLOCK" which attempts to find the last address of serious criminals wanted by local police departments. For about $100 per name, SHERLOCK will search the credit bureau's data base to find the wanted person.

People attempting to escape a bad credit history usually try a few predictable ploys. One of them is to transpose their middle and first names, while leaving everything else the same. This does not work because the credit bureau computer matches many more personal identifiers than just the name. If only this one item is changed, the computer will merge this into the pre-existing bad credit report. A simple attempt like this will often result in an alert being flashed across the face of the credit report telling the potential creditor to be careful. People also try the same thing by changing only the Social Security number and nothing else. As we have already seen, this strategy will frequently fail.

Let's look at TRW's fraud detection system. When a credit report on TRW's system detects a person attempting to leave behind a poor credit history, it flashes a "CHECKPOINT" warning across the screen. When a name variation or Social Security number change is attempted, the checkpoint message tells the creditor exactly this. One checkpoint message will indicate that the name given is a potential alias, another will tell the creditor that the Social Security number given is not accurate.

The Trans Union credit bureau system works a little differently. It is designed to look for small differences between the information given on the application and information the bureau already has on file. For example, some people seeking to jettison a poor credit history believe that by using a different address they can leave their old credit file behind. The Trans Union system will flag the new address and tell the creditor that it does not match what is now in the file.

These two systems are designed to detect the obvious. Some applicants have attempted to go much further than this however. For example, one ploy is to use the address and telephone number of a commercial mail receiving service. There was a time when this would have been enough to separate a person from their old credit history, but no longer. Because so many people have attempted to do this, all of the major credit bureaus have compiled listings of mail forwarding services and their telephone numbers. The same is true of telephone answering services. One of these addresses will immediately cause a warning to be flashed across the credit report.

Another step the credit bureaus have taken to protect themselves is to compile a listing of all Social Security numbers of deceased people, and to find out from the federal government which series of Social Security numbers are actively being issued. This cooperation between the Social Security Administration and the credit world reached a peak in 1989 when it was reported that the Social Security Administration was routinely verifying Social Security numbers for credit bureaus. The resulting uproar led to the dismissal of the then head of the Social Security Administration and a ban on this practice of wholesale number verification.

Another factor which sets off these credit bureau anti-fraud programs is a lot of credit inquiries in a very short period of time. All credit bureau systems will flag an excessive number of inquiries, and this will be flashed across the face of the report. This is because people with bad credit frequently use a scattershot approach, applying to many creditors over a short period of time hoping that one application will be approved.

These are some of the internal programs credit bureaus use to catch the poor credit applicant trying to leave his past behind. But this is only half of the picture. To obtain credit you must not only get past the credit bureau, you also must get approval from the creditors themselves. In the next chapter, we will go through a credit application one step at a time to see what creditors are looking for.

6
Step-By-Step Through The Credit Application

If you can successfully create a blank credit report, and you can induce a creditor to verify your employment and other references, the odds are very good that you will be approved for credit. We need to go through each item on a typical credit application and see what the creditor is looking for. The creditor will be looking for any inconsistencies or irregularities on the form. Any one variation is not likely to trigger a rejection, but a combination of several unusual entries may be cause for rejection.

Address Information

The first part of the application deals with the address information. Your address should always read as a street address to a house or have an apartment number specified. Frequently, when people use a mail forwarding service, they use a suite number to avoid writing a box number. Creditors are aware of this and the use of a suite number on a single-family street address may trigger the fraud detection software. The address should be complete, including the zip code. Absence of a zip code can trigger these programs, and an incorrect zip code will almost certainly cause suspicion. What person does not know his or her correct zip code?

Name and Professional Titles

The next part of the application to look at is the name and title. You must pay particular attention to these if you have created a new credit file as a professional person. There are certain conventions that professional people use when filling out their names and titles on applications or forms of any type. Most of these are common sense. For example, medical doctors do not write just the abbreviation "Dr." before their name; they almost always write "M.D." after their name.

The same goes for nurses and other professional medical personnel. Their academic or professional qualifications will almost always follow after their name. Engineers will often use the abbreviation "R.E." after their names to indicate they are licensed professional engineers. Nurses will write either "R.N." or "L.P.N." after their names. This also applies to professionals such as accountants, counselors, lawyers and others with academic degrees below the Ph.D. level. You need to pay close attention to the details.

Social Security Number

The next item in the personal information section is the Social Security number. Avoid the obvious mistakes. A Social Security number has nine digits, and no Social Security number starts higher than six, and no Social Security number has the middle two digits zero zero. Refer to the chart in Appendix 6 for more information on how the Social Security number should look for each state.

Date of Birth

The next item is your date of birth. Your date of birth should be consistent with the background you are portraying. This may seem obvious, but many fraudulent credit applicants are caught on this point. If your background is that of a college graduate with five years work experience, your age should reflect this. Your age on the application should be at least twenty seven. The programs supplied to credit grantors by the major bureaus provide age profiles that a creditor can check for a variety of careers.

Previous Addresses

After these items, most applications will ask for a previous address. This address should be a real address, complete with zip code. Do not be tempted to use a mail drop address for this address. One way to find a suitable previous address is simply to consult the telephone book and pull the name of someone at random from the book.

Use this person's address as your previous address. Make sure that you then consult the zip code directory to ensure that you have the correct zip code to match this address. This is a very important detail. Frequently, the applicant will have carefully prepared the rest of the application, but have not given any thought to the question of a previous address. Once again, it is the small details that the fraud programs look for.

Drivers License Number

The next spot to concentrate on is your drivers license number. Most credit applications will ask for your license number and state of issuance. Care must be exercised here as well. Most states use some simple coding system to assign license numbers. The remainder issue a simple sequential license number, or use the Social Security number as the license number. The creditor does not attempt to actually verify the number. What he attempts to do is to make sure that the number matches up to the state system for numbering licenses. If it does not, this will be another warning sign that can cause rejection.

Most large creditors have a copy of the book *I.D. Checking Guide*. This book provides an illustration of every state's drivers license, along with the numbering system they use. I recommend you obtain a copy if this item is difficult for you.

Employment History

The next part of the credit application we want to look at is the employment history and salary. Once again, you must pay close attention to ensure that your application falls within the accepted norms for the occupation that you have chosen. We should digress a moment and look at the whole area of employment and how creditors analyze it.

Creditors look at three primary facets of a person's employment. The first is what type of an occupation a person has. Creditors prefer a professional person or someone who works in a skilled trade. They prefer this type of occupation because it indicates long term job stability and increasing earning capacity over the years. Failing this, creditors prefer unionized workers who are employed by well established firms. On the other hand, a non-unionized worker employed at a growing company is preferable to a unionized employee at a factory with a history of layoffs.

Certain occupations are a no-no to creditors. Occupations such as waitresses, motel employees, etc., turn off creditors because of the high turnover in these jobs. For the applicant with an established credit history, the type of occupation is not so important. But to the blank slate credit seeker, it is critical. Lists of favorable and unfavorable occupations appear in Appendixes 3 and 4.

Most credit applications will ask for employer name, address, work telephone number, supervisor name, your job title, years of service, and your income. Your employer address should be a street address. I suggest that you arrange this through a secretarial service if you cannot provide a legitimate reference. What is most important is that your income match the range of someone typically employed in that industry with the same amount of experience. These figures can be obtained quite readily.

For professional occupations you can find average compensation levels from the appropriate professional society in your state. For workers at a unionized corporation you can obtain the salary scale by calling the union local that represents the workers at the plant concerned. Other occupational salary levels can be best ascertained by making inquiries to businesses that employ people in your stated occupation.

You need to pay close attention to the amount you write down for your salary. Never write a number that ends in zeros. For example, a salary of twenty thousand dollars per year seems odd. Consider your own income or those of people you know. People have wages that on a yearly or monthly basis end in funny amounts. Make sure the salary you list does the same. Another trap on some credit applications is they ask for your after tax income and not your gross income. Creditors that request after tax income have withholding tables and know how much net income a typical earner will have. You can do the same by obtaining a tax withholding table from Uncle Sam.

Financial Information

The next part of the application will deal with your financial status. This section must also be completed with close attention to detail to avoid triggering fraud programs. This section will ask such questions as the name and address of your financial institution, what type of accounts you have, their numbers and balances.

Let us look at what creditors actually do with this information. In general, creditors do not call your bank to verify these accounts. That would be too expensive and time consuming, and often banks will not release any information about an account in good standing to outside inquiries. Rather, the creditor will use fraud detection software to look for certain common patterns.

All creditors have access to a book that lists the names and addresses of all financial institutions in the United States. Most creditors also know which banks serve a given region. So the first caution is to give the name of an actual bank that operates where you claim to be living. The second place to be careful is in the account numbers you use. Banks and financial institutions generally issue seven digit account numbers. Look at your own checking and savings account numbers before you fill out the application. Use these as a guide.

Landlord Information

Landlord data is the next section you must deal with. Once again this can be handled relatively simply. What creditors are looking for here is a lack of information. Often new credit seekers will leave this section blank, hoping to slip through the net. The answer is very easy. If you are using a secretarial service as your landlord, simply provide the name and address of the service. What creditors are looking for is negative information. Most landlords do not report tenant payment histories to the credit bureau unless they are negative.

Credit History

The next section involves the credit history itself. This section must be filled out very carefully, and it can also be manipulated to your advantage. Let's see how to handle this section.

First of all, you want to be able to list something under this section. There are many credit accounts a person could have that do not report to the credit bureau. One example is book and record clubs where you order merchandise by mail and pay for it later on. These are credit transactions because the merchandise is shipped first and you are billed later on. These clubs do not report to credit bureaus as a general rule. So you can include these as credit references and not have it be suspicious that they don't appear on your credit report.

Another type of credit account you can set up is through mail order catalog shops. You will see advertisements from time to time in magazines that say something like "gold card with two thousand dollar limit available with no credit check." The way these operations work is you must pay an "account establishing fee" of between twenty and one hundred dollars. Once you have done this they will send you a catalog and a credit card that has your account number on it. When you order from the catalog you provide this number and the merchandise is shipped. You have the option of extended payments over time with a finance charge, or one payment in full for the balance. These companies will agree to provide you with a written credit statement after a few months of good payments.

You may be wondering how they can afford to ship merchandise to people they do not have any information on? First of all the quality of the goods in the catalog is very poor: cheap calculators, watches, radios, etc. The prices are usually three times as high as a local discount store, and the shipping and handling charges come on top of this. The shipping charges must be paid for in advance, and often these charges alone account for more than the true value of the goods ordered. Between the cost of the catalog and the charges for shipping and handling, the company has already earned a healthy profit before the order. The payments are pure profit. If a person defaults a few months down the line, the company has already made its money.

These companies can be listed on a credit application as credit references. Even though they do not ordinarily report accounts to the credit bureaus, they will provide you with a letter that you can enclose with your application verifying your account.

7
Becoming A Credit Card Millionaire

A few years ago on late-night television there was one of those 60-minute commercials that told how a person could become a millionaire using credit cards. Essentially, the upshot of the program was that a person could accumulate unlimited numbers of credit cards, and then by staggering the payment due dates, have up to 6 months free credit on the cards. Although that method is no longer workable, it is still possible to become rich using credit.

By accumulating, let's say, $40,000 in credit card credit lines, you allow yourself great flexibility. Perhaps you would like to purchase a new car without having a lien placed against the title. By taking cash advances on your credit cards you could do just this. Perhaps you want to start your own small business and lack capital. Most banks will not lend money to start new ventures.

Or perhaps you would like to purchase some property free and clear. Now you can. Regardless of what it is, it can be possible. The only drawback is that the interest rates charged on credit cards are so high, but later in this chapter I will show you how to convert that debt into low-interest long term debt that you can manage much more easily.

Start With a Blank Slate

We will assume that you have used the knowledge in this book to create a clear credit history for yourself and that you have obtained one secured VISA card and the credit union loan mentioned before. Once again the secret lies at the credit bureau.

One of the laws regulating credit bureaus says that an individual has the right to dispute at any time any entry on their credit file. When this is done, the credit bureau must furnish written verification to the individual concerned of the existence of the debt. If this isn't done within a "reasonable period of time," usually 60 days, the credit bureau must remove the entry from the credit report. Even if verification arrives later on, the credit bureau cannot re-insert the entry.

This is relevant because, as a way to prevent people from obtaining large amounts of unsecured credit, credit bureaus began keeping records of all credit report inquiries. Usually a credit report will list all credit inquiries within the last year. If a potential creditor sees a lot of inquiries within a given period of time, he will automatically deny credit.

This is how people who have no previous credit history can destroy their chances of getting credit. They apply time after time, not aware that each application is slowly destroying their ability to get credit later on. The question in each later creditor's mind is, "Why should I issue credit when the others did not?" Usually more than five inquiries within a year's time is enough to spoil any further credit extensions. So how do you get credit without having the inquiries show on your report?

Binging and Purging

The first step after you have gotten a secured credit card and a credit union loan is to apply for one of those very high interest rate credit cards offered by the big national banks. You see their advertisements in airports, hotels, and restaurants all over the country. You should apply for at least two of these cards. The reason for this is that it's easier to get a high-interest credit card than a low-interest one. The high interest rate combined with the annual fee allows the card issuer to lower its credit standards. The higher interest and annual fees ensure that the cards are very profitable even with the higher amount of losses incurred. With your clean credit report and two good credit references, these banks will gladly extend you a credit card with a substantial limit of $1,500 to $2,000. After you have these two cards, you must purge your credit report of these inquiries.

The law says you can write to any office of the credit bureau and request verification of the items on your credit report. So you would write to offices of the credit bureaus located far away from the creditors involved. A large bank will not waste time verifying an inquiry on an account that is paid up. For any inquiries that didn't result in credit being given —a rejection — the chances are slight that the bank will verify the inquiry. This method can be used time and time again to clean your credit report. The form letters for disputing an inquiry are shown in Chapter 3.

Some pointers you must keep in mind when doing this are that you must contact offices of all four major credit bureaus. Cleaning up your file at one credit bureau does not get a clean file at another credit bureau. Some times of year are better for doing this than others. This method works especially well in late October or early November because credit grantors heavily solicit new accounts at this time. It is almost guaranteed that the credit bureau's request for verification will be tossed in the garbage then. Early November is also an excellent time to apply for credit cards as lending standards are very relaxed to get people to go into debt for Christmas.

So you can proceed in this fashion to collect credit cards with high limits, then have the inquiries purged from your credit report, then go after more cards, then more purging, and on and on. Eventually, you will have access to tens of thousands of dollars in cash, possibly even hundreds of thousands. But it will be very expensive cash.

Converting to Low-Interest Debt

Once you have obtained this large amount of credit card debt, and purchased whatever you wanted, you will want to replace it with manageable long term debt. Let us assume that you purchased a new car for $11,000 and some bare land for $25,000. These are now assets. With these assets and your excellent credit report you could go to banks and apply for unsecured personal credit lines. These credit lines have much lower interest rates than credit cards and allow you to extend repayment over a longer term. Normally they are only available to the most credit worthy customers; you are one of the most credit worthy customers.

Usually these credit lines are from $2,000 to $5,000 apiece. You would then use these credit lines to pay off your high-interest credit cards. You could then shop around for very low-interest credit cards and get these to replace the high interest ones. Now your debt is even more manageable. This is especially so if you have started a new business with your credit.

You will still have to pay off all your debts some day. But we live in a society where those who can least afford it must pay the highest rates for credit, and those who don't need credit can get it for next to nothing. The secret to getting ahead in this society is getting access to low-interest capital. Using the method described above, you can accumulate a huge amount of capital to invest, and then convert all your debt to the low-rate, inexpensive variety. Then you will always have access to low-interest credit that can aid you in whatever you want to do.

Appendix One

Flowchart For New Credit

Step 1. Read this book.

Step 2. Request a copy of your current credit report from credit bureaus in your area.

Step 3. Open an alternate mailing address at a secretarial service or office rental service.

Step 4. Create a new dummy credit file using the procedure outlined.

Step 5. Request a copy of your new credit file to verify its content.

Step 6. Open up new checking and savings accounts based on the new information contained in your new credit file.

Step 7. Join a local credit union and open up a savings account.

Step 8. Apply for a secured mastercard or visa card account.

Step 9. Apply for a loan at credit union backed by your savings account as collateral.

Step 10. Pay off credit union loan account in two months.

Step 11. Apply for store or oil company charge account.

Appendix Two Secured VISA And Mastercard Account Programs

Key Federal Savings Bank
153 Chestnut Hill Road
Newark, Delaware 19713

New Era Bank
P.O. Box 15414
Wilmington, Delaware 19850

Pioneer First Federal Savings
4111 200th Street S.W.
Lynnwood, Washington 98036

Service One
Suite 215, 21032 Devonshire
Chatsworth, California 91311

Citicorp Savings of Illinois
P.O. Box 87581
Chicago, Illinois 60680

Berthoud National Bank
P.O. Box 3057
Omaha, Nebraska 68103

First Consumers National Bank
P.O. Box 2088
Portland, Oregon 97208

Appendix Three Employment Not Liked By Credit Grantors

Actors, unless well-known
Bartenders
Freelance writers
Local police officers
Motel or hotel employees, unless management
Restaurant workers, unless manager
Taxi drivers
Musicians, unless with well-known orchestra
General laborers, unless at a unionized company
Students, unless applying under a student program
Most self-employed people
Domestic workers
Barbers and beauticians
Non-degreed hospital workers

Appendix Four Occupations Liked By Creditors

Engineers with degrees

All types of technicians that require two years of higher education

Physicians

Registered nurses

All other professional allied health workers

Federal government employees

State or municipal government employees

All university teaching faculty and university support staff

Professional pilots with major airline or with regional airline

Unionized general laborers or factory workers with major company

Secretarial and data processing employees
Business management professionals

Appendix Five

Beating Credit Scoring Systems

Every bank uses a slightly different credit scoring system. By following the guidelines given here, you will be able to pass most systems.

1. Always have a telephone number listed in your name, or at least claim to. Often, the number provided is not verified.
2. Always indicate that you have lived at your current residence for at least three years.
3. Never list more than three dependents.
4. Always show at least four years employment with your current employer.
5. Always show at least five years or more at your previous address, if application asks about that.

6. Always make sure your monthly payments (not including rents) total less that 25% of your gross income.
7. Always list both a checking account and a savings account.

Appendix Six

Social Security Numbering System

Alabama	416-424	Kentucky	400-407
Alaska	574	Louisiana	433-439
Arizona	526-527	Maine	004-007
Arkansas	429-432	Maryland	212-220
California	545-573	Massachusetts	010-034
Colorado	521-524	Michigan	362-386
Connecticut	040-049	Minnesota	468-477
Delaware	221-222	Mississippi	425-428
D.C.	577-579	Missouri	486-500
Florida	261-267	Montana	516-517
Georgia	252-260	Nebraska	505-508
Hawaii	575-576	Nevada	530
Idaho	518-519	New Hampshire	001-003
Illinois	318-361	New Jersey	135-158
Indiana	303-317	New Mexico	525 & 585
Iowa	478-485	New York	050-134
Kansas	509-515	North Carolina	237-246

North Dakota	501-502
Ohio	268-302
Oklahoma	440-448
Oregon	540-544
Pennsylvania	159-211
Rhode Island	035-039
South Carolina	247-251
South Dakota	503-504
Tennessee	408-415
Texas	449-467
Utah	528-529
Vermont	008-009
Virginia	223-231
Washington	531-539
West Virginia	223-231
Wisconsin	387-399
Wyoming	520

Additions

Arizona	600-601
California	602-626
Florida	589-595
Mississippi	587-588
New Mexico	585
North Carolina	232

Miscellaneous

Virgin Islands	580
Puerto Rico	580-584
Guam, Samoa & Pacific Terr.	586
Railroad Ret.	700-728

Appendix Seven

Additional Sources Of Information

Reborn in the U.S.A.
by Trent Sands
Published by Loompanics Unlimited
P.O. Box 1197
Port Townsend, WA 98368

Credit: The Cutting Edge
by Scott French
Published by Paladin Press
P.O. Box 1307
Boulder, CO 80306

Credit Secrets
by Bob Hammond
Published by Paladin Press

Credit Mechanic
by J. Arlene White
Published by Paladin Press

Credit Card Fraud
by Burt Rapp
Published by Loompanics Unlimited